Oxford Universi

Super Songs

◆ Songs for very young learners ◆

Hello

Illustrated by Alex Ayliffe, Peter Stevenson
and Rowan Barnes-Murphy

عنوان و نام پدیدآور: Super Songs: Songs for Very Young Learners/ Illustrated by Alex Ayliffe, Peter Stevenson and Rowan Barnes - Murphy

مشخصات نشر: تهران: رهنما، ۱۳۹۳ = ۲۰۱٤م.

مشخصات ظاهری: ۳۲ ص،: و زیری

وضعیت فهرست‌نویسی: فیپا

یادداشت: انگلیسی

آوانویسی عنوان: سوپر...

موضوع: زبان انگلیسی– راهنمای آموزشی – وسایل کمک آموزشی دیداری و شنیداری

موضوع: زبان انگلیسی – – راهنمای آموزشی (ابتدایی)

موضوع: ترانه‌های انگلیسی

شناسه افزوده: آیلیف، الکس، تصویرگر

شناسه افزوده: Ayliffe, Alex

شناسه افزوده: استیونسون، پیتر، ۱۹۵۳ – م، تصویرگر

شناسه افزوده: Stevenson, Peter

شناسه افزوده: بارنز- مورفی، روون، ۱۹۵۲ – م، تصویرگر

شناسه افزوده: Barnes - Murphy, Rowan

ردهبندی کنگره: PE۱۰۶۷/ م۹ ۱۳۹۳

ردهبندی دیویی: ٤۲۸/۰۰۷۱

شماره کتابشناسی ملی: ۳٤۹۳۹۲٦

Super Songs، مؤلفین: Alex Ayliffe و Peter Stevenson و Rowan Barnes-Murphy، چاپ: چاپخانه نقره‌فام، چاپ اول: ۱۳۹۳، تیراژ: ۱۰۰۰ نسخه، ناشر: انتشارات رهنما آدرس: مقابل دانشگاه تهران، خیابان فروردین، نبش خیابان شهدای ژاندارمری، پلاک ۱۱۲، تلفن: ۶۶۴۰۰۹۲۷، ۶۶۴۱۶۶۰۴، ۶۶۴۸۱۶۶۲، فاکس: ۶۶۴۶۷۲۲۳ فروشگاه رهنما، سعادت‌آباد، خیابان علامه طباطبایی جنوبی، بین ۳۰ و ۳۲ شرقی، پلاک ۲۹، تلفن: ۸۸۶۹۳۱۰۲، ۸۸۶۹۴۱۰۲ آدرس فروشگاه شماره ۴: خیابان پیروزی نبش خیابان سوم نیروی هوایی، تلفن: ۷۷۳۸۲۵۰۵، نمایشگاه کتاب رهنما، مقابل دانشگاه تهران پاساژ فروزنده، تلفن: ۶۶۹۵۰۹۵۷

قیمت: ۴۰۰۰۰ ریال

CONTENTS

Five currant buns in a baker's shop,
Round and fat with sugar on the top.
Along came a boy with a penny one day,
Bought a currant bun and took it away.

Four currant buns . . .
Three currant buns . . .
Two currant buns . . .

One currant bun in a baker's shop,
Round and fat with sugar on the top.
Along came a boy with a penny one day,
Bought the currant bun and took it away.

Five currant buns . . .

Round and fat

with sugar
on the top.

Along came a boy
with a penny one day,

Bought the
currant bun

and took it away.

8

4

THE WHEELS ON THE BUS

The wheels on the bus go round and round,
Round and round, round and round,
The wheels on the bus go round and round,
All day long.

The children on the bus go wriggle wriggle wriggle . . .

The mummies on the bus go 'Don't do that!'. . .

The daddies on the bus go read read read . . .

The babies on the bus go 'Wah wah wah!'. . .

The wheels on
the bus . . .

The children on
the bus . . .

The mummies on
the bus . . .

The daddies on
the bus . . .

The babies on
the bus . . .

5

Here We Go Looby-Loo

Chorus:
Here we go Looby-Loo,
Here we go Looby-Light,
Here we go Looby-Loo,
All on a Saturday night.

Put your right hand in,
Put your right hand out,
Shake it a little, a little,
And turn yourself about.

(Chorus)

Put your left hand in . . .

(Chorus)

Put your right foot in . . .

(Chorus)

Put your left foot in . . .

(Chorus)

Put your whole self in . . .

(Chorus)

| *Here we go looby-Loo . . .* | Put your right hand in. | Put your right hand out. | Shake it a little. a little. | And turn yourself about |

TWO LITTLE EYES

Two little eyes to look around,
Two little ears to hear each sound,
One little nose to smell what's sweet,
One little mouth that likes to eat.

Two little eyes . . .   Two little ears . . .   One little nose . . .   One little mouth . . .

7

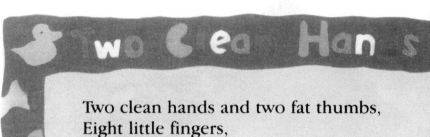

Two Clean Hands

Two clean hands and two fat thumbs,
Eight little fingers,
Ten little toes,
One round head goes nod, nod, nodding,
Two eyes peeping,
One tiny nose.

Two clean hands
and two fat thumbs.

Eight little fingers.

Ten little toes.

goes nod, nod,
nodding,

Two eyes
peeping,

One tiny nose.

HEAD, SHOULDERS KNEES AND TOES

Head, shoulders, knees, and toes,
Knees and toes,
Head, shoulders, knees, and toes,
Knees and toes.
Eyes and ears and mouth and nose,
Head, shoulders, knees and toes,
Knees and toes.

Head, shoulders, knees, and toes . . . Eyes and ears and mouth and nose . . .

Wind the bobbin up,
Wind the bobbin up,
Pull, pull, clap, clap, clap.
Point to the ceiling,
Point to the floor,
Point to the window,
Point to the door.
Clap your hands together,
One, two, three,
Put your hands down on your knee.

Wind the bobbin up . . .   Pull, pull.   clap, clap, clap.   Point to the ceiling,   Point to the floor,

Point to the window.   Clap your hands together,   One, two, three,   Put your hands down
Point to the door.   on your knee.

Jelly on a plate, jelly on a plate,
Wibble wobble, wibble wobble,
Jelly on a plate.

Sausages in a pan, sausages in a pan
Turn them over, turn them over,
Sausages in a pan.

Wibble wobble, wibble wobble . . .   Turn them over, turn them over . . .

11

Pat-a-cake, pat-a-cake,
Baker's man,
Bake me a cake
As fast as you can.
Pat it and prick it
And mark it with 'B'
And put it in the oven for baby and me.

Pat-a-cake, pat-a-cake . . .   Pat it and prick it   And mark it with 'B'   And put it in the oven . . .

CLAP YOUR HANDS

Clap your hands, clap your hands,
Clap them just like me.
Touch your shoulders, touch your shoulders,
Touch them just like me.

Tap your knees, tap your knees,
Tap them just like me.
Shake your head, shake your head,
Shake it just like me.
Clap your hands, clap your hands.
Then let them quiet be.

Touch your shoulders . . .   Shake your head . . .   Then let them quiet be.

Clap your hands . . .   Tap your knees . . .   Clap your hands . .

13

Ten Little Teddy Bears

One little, two little, three little teddy bears,
Four little, five little, six little teddy bears,
Seven little, eight little, nine little teddy bears,
Ten little teddy bears.

One little, two little . . .

TWO LITTLE DICKY BIRDS

Two little dicky birds
Sitting on a wall.
One named Peter,
One named Paul.

Fly away Peter,
Fly away Paul.
Come back Peter,
Come back Paul.

Two little
dicky birds . . .

One named
Peter . . .

Fly away Peter,

Fly away Paul.

Come back Peter,

Come back Paul.

TEN IN THE BED

There were ten in the bed
And the little one said,
'Roll over! Roll over!'
So they all rolled over
And one fell out . . .

There were nine . . .
There were eight . . .
There were seven . . .
There were six . . .
There were five . . .
There were four . . .
There were three . . .
There were two . . .

There was one in the bed
And no one said,
'Roll over! Roll over!'
So no one rolled over
And no one fell out!

So they all rolled over   And one fell out . . .

16

Five brown teddies

Five brown teddies sitting on a wall,
Five brown teddies sitting on a wall,
And if one brown teddy should accidentally fall,
There'd be four brown teddies sitting on the wall.

Four brown teddies sitting on a wall . . .

Three brown teddies sitting on a wall . . .

Two brown teddies sitting on a wall . . .

One brown teddy sitting on a wall,
One brown teddy sitting on a wall,
And if one brown teddy should accidentally fall,
There'd be no brown teddies sitting there at all!

Five brown teddies sitting on a wall . . .   And if one brown teddy should accidentally fall . . .

17

One potato, two potatoes,
Three potatoes, four,
Five potatoes, six potatoes,
Seven potatoes, more.

18

IT'S RAINING, IT'S POURING

It's raining, it's pouring,
The old man is snoring.
He went to bed and bumped his head
And couldn't get up in the morning.

It's raining, it's pouring,   The old man is snoring.   He went to bed and
                                                          bumped his head . . .

Red and yellow
And pink and green,
Purple and orange and blue.
I can sing a rainbow,
Sing a rainbow,
Sing a rainbow, too.

INCY WINCY SPIDER

Incy Wincy Spider climbed up the spout.
Down came the rain and washed poor Incy out.
Out came the sun and dried up all the rain.
Incy Wincy Spider climbed the spout again.

Incy Wincy Spider
climbed up the spout.   Down came the rain . . .   Out came the sun . . .   Incy Wincy Spider
climbed the spout again.

21

Tall shops in the town.
Lifts going up and down.
Doors going in and out.
People walking all about.

Tall shops in the town. Lifts going up and down. Doors going in and out. People walking all about.

MISS POLLY HAD A DOLLY

Miss Polly had a dolly who was sick, sick, sick,
So she phoned for the doctor to come quick, quick, quick.
The doctor came with her bag and her hat,
And she knocked at the door with a rat-a-tat-tat.

She looked at the dolly and she shook her head,
And she said, 'Miss Polly, put her straight to bed.'
She wrote on a paper for a pill, pill, pill,
'I'll be back in the morning with my bill, bill, bill.'

Miss Polly had a dolly . . .   So she phoned for the doctor . . .   The doctor came with her bag and her hat.   And she knocked at the door . . .

She looked at the dolly and she shook her head,   And she said, 'Miss Polly, put her straight to bed.'   She wrote on a paper . . .   'I'll be back in the morning . . .'

Oh, we can play the big bass drum
And this is the way we do it.
BOOM, BOOM, BOOM, goes the big bass drum
And that's the way we do it.

Oh, we can play the violin . . .
FIDDLE-DIDDLE-DEE, goes the violin . . .

Oh, we can play the triangle . . .
TING, TING, TING, goes the triangle . . .

Oh, we can play the silver flute . . .
TOOTLE-OOTLE-OOT, goes the silver flute . . .

Oh, we can play the big bass drum . . .

Oh, we can play the violin . . .

Oh, we can play the triangle . . .

Oh, we can play the silver flute . . .

24

Ladybird, Ladybird

Ladybird, ladybird, fly away home,
Your house is on fire and your children are gone.
All except one; her name is Anne,
And she has crept under the frying-pan.

IN A COTTAGE IN A WOOD

In a cottage in a wood,
A little man at the window stood.
He saw a rabbit running by,
Knocking at the door.

'Help me, help me,' the rabbit said,
'Before the hunter shoots me dead!'

'Come little rabbit, come with me.
Happy we shall be.'

In a cottage in a wood.   A little man at the window stood   He saw a rabbit running by.   Knocking at the door.

'Help me. help me. the rabbit said.   'Before the hunter shoots me dead!   'Come little rabbit, come with me.   Happy we shall be.'

Twinkle, Twinkle, Little Star

Twinkle, twinkle, little star,
How I wonder what you are.
Up above the world so high
Like a diamond in the sky.
Twinkle, twinkle, little star,
How I wonder what you are.

Twinkle, twinkle, little star,

How I wonder what you are.

Up above the world so high

Like a diamond in the sky . . .

27

O Christmas tree, O Christmas tree,
How lovely are your branches.
O Christmas tree, O Christmas tree,
How lovely are your branches.

In summer sun or winter snow
A coat of green you always show.
O Christmas tree, O Christmas tree,
How lovely are your branches.

O Christmas tree . . .   In summer sun   or winter snow   A coat of green you
always show.

A Witch Came Flying

A witch came flying, flying, flying,
A witch came flying, flying, flying,
A witch came flying all on a summer's day.

A clown came dancing, dancing, dancing . . .

A king came marching, marching, marching . . .

A wolf came running, running, running . . .

A witch came flying . .

A clown came dancing . . .

A king came marching . . .

A wolf came running . . .

29

Oxford University Press,
Great Clarendon Street,
Oxford OX2 6DP

Oxford • New York
Athens • Auckland • Bangkok • Bogota
Bombay • Buenos Aires • Calcutta • Cape Town
Dar es Salaam • Delhi • Florence • Hong Kong
Istanbul • Karachi • Kuala Lumpur • Madras
Madrid • Melbourne • Mexico City • Nairobi • Paris
Singapore • Taipei • Tokyo • Toronto

and associated companies in
Berlin • Ibadan

OXFORD and OXFORD ENGLISH
are trade marks of Oxford University Press

ISBN 0 19 433625 5

Printed in Hong Kong

Acknowledgements

Sing a rainbow (Arthur Hamilton)
© 1955 Mark VII Ltd, WB Music Corp, USA
Warner/Chappell Music Ltd, London W1Y 3FA
Reproduced by permission of International Music Publications Ltd

Tall Shops
© 1933 Stainer & Bell Ltd, London, England

Designed by Mo Choy